George Melville Baker

# One Hundred Years Ago

Our Boys of 1776

George Melville Baker

**One Hundred Years Ago**
*Our Boys of 1776*

ISBN/EAN: 9783337307233

Printed in Europe, USA, Canada, Australia, Japan

Cover: Foto ©Thomas Meinert / pixelio.de

More available books at **www.hansebooks.com**

# ONE HUNDRED YEARS AGO;

OR,

## OUR BOYS OF 1776.

*A PATRIOTIC DRAMA IN TWO ACTS.*

BY THE AUTHOR OF

"Sylvia's Soldier," "Once on a Time," "Down by the Sea," "Bread on the Waters," "The Last Loaf," "Stand by the Flag," "The Tempter," "A Drop Too Much," "We're All Teetotalers," "A Little More Cider," "Thirty Minutes for Refreshments," "Wanted, a Male Cook," "A Sea of Troubles," "Freedom of the Press," "A Close Shave," "The Great Elixir," "The Man with the Demijohn," "New Brooms Sweep Clean," "Humors of the Strike," "My Uncle the Captain," "The Greatest Plague in Life," "No Cure, No Pay," "The Grecian Bend," "The War of the Roses," "Lightheart's Pilgrimage," "The Sculptor's Triumph," "Too Late for the Train," "Snow-Bound," "The Peddler of Very Nice," "Bonbons," "Capuletta," "An Original Idea," "Enlisted for the War," "Never say Die," "The Champion of her Sex," "The Visions of Freedom," "The Merry Christmas of the Old Woman who lived in a Shoe," "The Tournament of Idylcourt," "A Thorn among the Roses," "A Christmas Carol," &c.

BOSTON:

GEORGE M. BAKER AND COMPANY,

41-45 FRANKLIN STREET.

1876.

# ONE HUNDRED YEARS AGO;

## OR, OUR BOYS OF 1776.

### A PATRIOTIC DRAMA IN TWO ACTS.

---

## CHARACTERS.

OBED STERLING, a Quaker.
EPHRAIM STERLING, his Son.
ELMER GRANGER, a Young Patriot.
URIEL BOSWORTH, a Quaker Convert.
PRETZEL, a Dutchman.
GINGER, a Negro.
BURKE, } Tories.
BLUCHER, }
RACHEL STERLING, the Quaker Mother.
RUTH STERLING, her Daughter.
PRUDENCE GRANGER, Elmer's Sister.

The scene of the drama is near Philadelphia, July 4, 1776.

---

## COSTUMES.

OBED.   Black, brown, or gray Quaker suit; white hair, parted
in centre; long stockings, to match suit; plain black shoes;
broad-brimmed hat.

BOSWORTH and EPHRAIM.   Quaker suits of same character, but
differing in color or in the color of stockings.   Bosworth has
black hair, parted in middle; Ephraim a very light wig, parted
in the middle, with hair slightly curly at ends.

**ELMER.**  Neat suit of continental fashion; brown coat; buff vest; white necktie; brown breeches; blue stockings; shoes with buckles; cocked hat.

**PRETZEL.**  Brown trunks, or full trousers fastened at the knee; blue stockings; short brown coat; small Dutch cap, or knit woollen cap with tassel at end.

**GINGER.**  Gray breeches; red stockings; blue striped shirt; red waistcoat, open; grizzled wig; heavy shoes.

**BLUCHER** and **BURKE.**  Brown coats; red waistcoats; dark breeches; brown or gray stockings; shoes without buckles.

**MRS. STERLING.**  Gray dress; white kerchief, neatly pinned across bosom; Quaker cap.

**RUTH.**  Brown or gray dress, opening in front, showing white skirt, rather short; long sleeves; high neck; white hose, and black shoes; hair light, in Grecian knot.

**PRUDENCE.**  Short patch petticoat, with looped overskirt and waist of red material; sleeves rolled up in first act, and apron on; hair done up high with large comb; sleeves turned down for second act.

The Quaker costumes may be hard to obtain, but can easily be manufactured.  For hats, cover wide-rimmed straw hats with brown or gray cambric, "wrong-side" out.  For coats, "stand up" the collars of any old-fashioned dark coats, to give a prim and stiff appearance.  The balance can easily be obtained.  Guns used in this piece should have the *appearance* of flint-locks.

## STAGE DIRECTIONS.

R., right; C., centre; L., left; L C., left centre; R. C., right centre; L. 1 E., left first entrance; R. 1 E., right first entrance; FLAT, scene at back of stage; R. U. E., right upper entrance.

# ONE HUNDRED YEARS AGO;

OR,

## OUR BOYS OF 1776.

———◆———

*A PATRIOTIC DRAMA IN TWO ACTS.*

ACT I. — MORNING. *Kitchen in Obed Sterling's house.
Door in flat* R. C. *Window in flat* L. C., *with muslin
curtain draped. Fireplace* R., *with fire burning, and
teakettle hanging on crane. Door or entrance* L. 1 E.,
R. 1 E., *and* R. U. E. *Settle* R., *between fire and
door. (If this cannot be easily procured, form one
by placing two wooden chairs side by side, and cover
with cotton cloth.)* L. C., *near window, tub on wooden
bench, partly filled with suds, washboard, and white
clothes, piece of yellow soap on washboard, clothes-
basket and pail on floor beside tub. Table* L., *against
scene, chair* R. *of it. Add any old-fashioned things,
such as spinning-wheel, churn, &c., that may be pro-
curable, and place out of the way at* R. *or* L. *As the
curtain rises, drum and fife are heard playing
"Yankee Doodle" outside, gradually dying away in
the distance.* PRUDENCE *discovered at window, holding back curtain, and looking out.*

1*                                                          5

*Prudence.* There they go. Bless their true, loyal hearts! I wish King George could only see them. He'd need but one look at their stout forms and brave faces to teach him that all the Stamp Acts in creation.couldn't stamp out the grit that's ground into every mother's son that has rolled in this rugged soil. (*Turns to tub, and washes briskly.*) I'm glad to see this sojery here. It did look for a while as though the Tories were going to have it all their own way; but the patriots have woke up, and I reckon there'll be lively times here. It takes me right back to dear old Concord, and the day the British came up to surprise us. The drum and fife played to some purpose then. They came and found us ready, and the getting back a pesky sight harder than the coming. It was a sad day for us. Father fell among the first. Our old house was burned to the ground; and mother (it sickens me to think of it) was butchered by a coward. And, but for my brave brother, I — I — (*Puts hands to her eyes.*) Dear me! I've filled my eyes with suds. I won't think of that fearful scene. Many homes must be blasted before the tyrant can be made to feel he is powerless to enslave a people roused to a sense of their wrongs. Come, Prudence, chirk up. There's bluing enough in your tub; so don't you get the blues. (*Sings air " Yankee Doodle."*)

" Father and I went down to camp,
    Along of Capt. Tooding;
  And there we saw the men and boys,
    As thick as hasty pudding."

(*Enter* PRETZEL *door in flat, with pipe in his mouth;*

*leans against door-post, and smokes while she is singing the chorus.*)

> "Yankee doodle, keep it up,
>     Yankee doodle dandy;
>   Mind the music and the steps,
>     And with the girls be handy."

*Pretzel.* Yaw, dot is goot. Miss Prudence, vash you dare?

*Prudence.* Yes, Mr. Pretzel, I *wash* here.

*Pretzel.* Yaw. I hear you sing sometings. You hear der droms and der fifes ven der play 'long mit der music?

*Prudence.* Hear them? I should think so. That tune should wake the spirit of every man who loves his country.

*Pretzel.* Yaw, dot is so. It vake me right up from mine shleep, and I feel so mad dot I moost do sometings right avay pretty quick.

*Prudence.* For your country? You have a noble spirit, Mr. Pretzel.

*Pretzel.* Yaw, spirit is goot. I moost do sometings: so I call mine man Yawcup to go right avay and get me —

*Prudence.* Your gun. I see, noble Pretzel.

*Pretzel.* Right avay down cellar, and draw mine peer.

*Prudence.* Pshaw! you've got no patriotism.

*Pretzel.* Batriotism. I donno vhat you mean by dot; but I be got der pest peer —

*Prudence.* Is this the time to think of beer?

*Pretzel.* Yaw, der ish no time dot ever vas to come pefore dot I do not tink of mine peer.

*Prudence.*   'Tis out of place now.

*Pretzel.*   Nein : 'tis in der keg onder de stairs, first on der right as you go town mit der left.

*Prudence.*   I don't want to hear any more about your beer.

*Pretzel.*   Yaw.   Vell, I haf else sometings dot will blease you (*sits on settle*), — sometings dot make me so shtupid dot I can't shut mine eyes vhen I haf gone to shleep mit mine ped.   Dot is you, fraulein.   I loaf you.

*Prudence (with clothes in her hands, starts back : very loud).*   What?

*Pretzel.*   Yaw.   I loaf you petter dan sourkraut, petter dan mine peer.   Ven I tink of you mit your pright eyes, my heart joomp right out of mine mout, and peats droomsticks mit my posom.

*Prudence (snapping her teeth, and wringing out a sheet).*   It does, does it?

*Pretzel.*   Yaw.   So I get run ofer from mine house to get you for mine frau.   So you comes mit me, and be mine frau, and you shall vash all der day mit your tub, — all mine close dot never haf peen vashed at all some more.

*Prudence (who has twisted a wet sheet into a weapon).*   Mr. Pretzel, do you see that door?

*Pretzel (looks round at door without rising).*   Yaw ; dot is a goot toor.

*Prudence (comes down stage).*   Then instantly take yourself outside of it.

*Pretzel.*   Mit you, fraulein?

*Prudence (strikes pipe from his mouth with her*

*weapon*). Never, you mean, contemptible, cowardly Dutchman !

*Pretzel* (*jumping up*). Vhat for you smash mine pipe? You vant to proke mine heart mit your nonsense?

*Prudence.* I'll break your head if you're not out of this house quick. (*Flourishing her weapon.*) Go!

*Pretzel.* Keep avay! I'll bring you tamages mit a court; and I'll nefer come back here some more.

*Prudence.* If you do, I'll scald you. (*Threatening.*) Go!

*Pretzel* (*at door*). Yaw. May I nefer hope to die if I do. (*Exit door in flat.*)

*Prudence* (*returns to tub*). Was there ever such impudence? Ha, ha, ha! I've found a lover at last. Poor old Pretzel wants a frau. "You come mit me." Ha, ha, ha! I needn't die an old maid; but it will certainly be my last chance when I consent to become Frau Pretzel. (*Wrings out clothes, and puts them in basket. GINGER heard outside whistling "Yankee Doodle." He throws open door, and marches down stage to front, still whistling; has a heavy stick of wood at "shoulder-arms."*)

*Ginger* (*marking time*). Ker-ker-kerumpany — tension. Halt! order — hams! (*Lets stick down upon his toe; drops it, seizes foot with both hands, hops across stage on one foot howling, drops into chair, L.*) Whwh-what de infusion in de ranks? Whooh! — dar's a halt in de confield sure's you bawn.

*Prudence.* Ginger, where on earth have you been?

*Ginger.* Hm? Dat you, Miss Prudence? Been down

wid de sojers onto de — de pomade ground, you know, down de cow-pastur. Lots of 'em down dar, and so fine. Oh, golly! Dar was Cunnel Stuffin —

*Prudence.* No, no, Ginger: Col. Griffin.

*Ginger.* Hm? Wal, he had stuffin nuff in his buzzum to fill a bolster. Den dar was Capn — Capn Gingham.

*Prudence.* Oh, no, Ginger! Capt. Ingram.

*Ginger.* Yas, dat what I said, — Cap'n Gingham. He was dressed up fine, he was. He had a big shut — shut — shut — two on his head; an' — an' — an' — a yaller flume stuck into it; an' — an' — a red crash round his waist; an' — an' — a napkin on his back; an' — an' — a partridge-box fastened onto his side. Golly! he jes as proud as — as — a rooster in de barn-yard. Lots dere, Miss Prudence. I wanted to jine, but dey wouldn't let me. Said 'twould spoil my complex. Dey was going to trabble in de sun, and I'd get tanned. If some of dem fellows don't get tanned, den shoot *me.*

*Prudence.* It is a grand rising. I've seen many such down East.

*Ginger.* Down Yeast! Yas, dat's de yeast dat sets de whole country rising.

*Prudence.* Come, Ginger, help me with the basket.

*Ginger (rising).* To be sure, to be sure! (*Limps.*) Have jes' about smashed dat ere hoof (*feels of heel*); but de vital part am safe. (*Enter* Mrs. Sterling R. U. E., *with knitting in her hands.*)

*Mrs. S.* Has thee nearly finished thy washing, Prudence?

*Prudence.* Yes. The last basketful is just going out.

*Mrs. S.* Thee is a smart girl, Prudence, and a good one.

*Prudence.* And you are a good, kind friend to me; for when I had no home, out of love for my mother, who had left the Friends to marry my father, you called me to you, and comforted me in my sorrow with loving words and kind acts.

*Mrs. S.* Child, thee has repaid us a thousand-fold. Thy hands are skilful, thy feet active, thy whole soul is in thy work, and thy singing and laughter sunshine in our sober house.

*Ginger.* Dat's so, missus; she de sunshine in de garden too. De roses blush wid pleasure when she skips along de paths; an' — an' — de great proud sunflowers look ashamed of demselves for being so ugly looking; an' — an' de inyuns waft de fragrance; an' — an' —

*Prudence.* Ha, ha, ha! Ginger, you are too romantic.

*Ginger.* Got a little touch of de rumatics when dat ar stick dropped.

*Prudence.* Come, we shall not get the clothes out to-day. (*Takes handle of basket.*)

*Ginger* (*takes other side of basket*). Say, Miss Prudence, why am we — us, you and me — like twins?

*Prudence.* Can't guess that, Ginger.

*Ginger.* Kase — kase — kase we's so *clothesly* united. See? Yah, yah, yah! Dat's a conunderdone.

*Prudence.* It's overdone, Ginger; we must find a dividing line somewhere.

*Ginger.* We'll hab to trabble from pole to pole to find it. Yah, yah, yah! (*Exeunt* PRUDENCE *and* GINGER, *with basket, door in* F.)

*Mrs. S.* (*sitting on settle, and knitting*). She's a dear good girl, though she does plague the Friends with her plain talk on equal rights and liberty. They call her a firebrand; but I like her all the better for that. She is a spark thrown up by the great fire of patriotism which waved so grandly at Concord, fallen here to kindle a fresh blaze for liberty. Ah, Rachel! thee is a little treacherous to thy faith. The Friends counsel peace; but I fear thy heart is with the oppressed. (*Enter, door in flat,* OBED STERLING, *followed by* BOSWORTH.)

*Obed.* What thee says may be true, Friend Bosworth; but the Friends counsel neutrality in these troublous days.

*Bosworth.* Nay, nay; the Friends are wrong. We *must* take side in the coming struggle. Thee knows the rebels are in council now in the city, have already framed a declaration of independence which to-day will be adopted. Their harangues are loud and bitter. They hurl defiance at our good Friend George, who is the rightful owner of this soil. We must be just to him.

*Mrs. S.* Though he be unjust to us. Thinkest thou this would be the advice of Friend William Penn, who bought this land of Friend George, and gave it to us as a refuge from oppressors?

*Obed.* Nay nay, Rachel; thee must not counsel opposition. We are Friends. If our enemy smite us on the right cheek, we must turn to him the left.

*Mrs. S.* Verily, Obed, thee speaks not the words of soberness. When the tax-gatherer did smite thee on the cheek, thee did turn upon him with thy fist, and smite him to the ground.

*Obed.* Nay, speak not of that, Rachel. I did forget myself.

*Mrs. S.* Then let thy memory be treacherous again on the side of right and justice.

*Obed.* Nay, nay, it must not be. I should set a bad example to son Ephraim, who is strongly imbued with the principles of peace; and daughter Ruth — where is the child?

*Mrs. S.* I left her at her window tending plants.

*Obed.* Thee had better go to her. I thought I saw her, as I came in, with her eyes fastened upon the warlike evolutions of the rebels beyond. I fear the plants will be neglected.

*Mrs. S.* I will send her to thee and Friend Bosworth. (*Exit* R. U. E.)

*Obed.* Sit thee down, Friend Bosworth (*sits on settle*).

*Bosworth* (*takes chair from table, and sits* C.). Friend Obed, thy daughter is a comely damsel, and fair to look upon.

*Obed.* Yea, she is like the best fruits of my orchard, — fair and rosy to the eye, sound and wholesome to the core.

*Bosworth.* Thee will not think me presuming, Obed; for thee has been very kind to me. When I came to thee a stranger, thee did use thy influence with the Friends, and made me one of thy sect.

2

*Obed.* Yea, thee was a stranger, — one who had fled from persecution in Massachusetts, because thee would not join the unrighteous rebels in their opposition to Friend George. Yea, I did stand thy friend.

*Bosworth.* Thee can stand my friend again, if thee but choose. I love thy daughter Ruth.

*Obed.* Thee — thee love my daughter!

*Bosworth.* Yea, Friend Obed; give her to me, and thee will never regret it.

*Obed.* If daughter Ruth saith Yea to thy petition, thee will find me thy friend; but she shall make her own free choice.

*Bosworth.* Hearken, Friend Obed. In a few days this place will be filled with British soldiers. Only the friends of Friend George will be free from molestation. Should thee remain neutral, thy fine place will be despoiled, thy gold seized, thyself and thy friends be left homeless. Thee should prepare for this.

*Obed.* Prepare! How?

*Bosworth.* Make friends with the agents of Friend George. Offer thy services to assist in breaking down this unhallowed rebellion.

*Obed.* Offer my services! Don't thee forget I am a Friend, — forbidden to bear arms?

*Bosworth.* Thee need not, Friend Obed, bear arms. There are other ways in which thee can aid. I am in the service of Friend George.

*Obed.* Thee, Friend Bosworth?

*Bosworth.* Yea. When his soldiers come, I shall pass in a list of the loyal and the rebellious. The property of the rebels will be seized. The loyal will still hold their own.

*Obed.* Bosworth, thee is a spy.

*Bosworth.* Thee gives my poor services a hard name. No matter. These rebels shall suffer for the wrongs they have heaped upon me ; and I'll sell them body and soul, if craft and cunning can do it.

*Obed.* And thee would marry my daughter?

*Bosworth.* Would? I will. I am powerful now. I can denounce ; I can protect. If thee will use thy influence with her, I stand thy friend ; if not, thee and thy household must be outlawed. 'Tis a fair bargain. Her hand for thy peace, perhaps thy life.

*Obed.* Nay, thee knows 'tis my custom to sleep upon a bargain. Fear not ; thy offer shall be well considered. . Hush ! Here is daughter Ruth. (*Enter Ruth* R. U. E.)

*Ruth.* Mother tells me thee does want me, father.

*Obed.* Nay, daughter. I did but ask for thee, missing thee from the kitchen.

*Ruth.* Prudence sent me away. I would have helped her with the washing, but she bade me begone ; so I have been at my window, watering the plants.

*Obed.* And watching the men of war on the green.

*Ruth.* Yea, thee is right. My eyes would wander that way. Was I wrong? Thee has taught me that war is unholy ; that man has no right to take the life of his brother-man.

*Obed.* Thee has been taught well.

*Ruth.* Then Friend George across the water must be a very wicked man ; for 'twas by his order the first blood was shed.

*Obed.* Nay: he was but asserting his right to his own property.

*Ruth.* Then our neighbors do right in defending their liberties. Is it not so?

*Obed.* Nay, child; thee cannot understand this quarrel. Thee had better hold thy peace. Does thee not see Friend Bosworth?

*Ruth.* Friend Bosworth, thee is welcome.

*Bosworth.* Thee is always kind, Friend Ruth. And so thee has a wicked sympathy for these rebellious neighbors?

*Ruth.* Yea. I must be a very wicked little Quaker; for I do hope they will wax strong in their faith that liberty is a birthright; and he who would not defend it with his life is a coward. (*Turns up stage to window, and looks out.*)

*Bosworth.* Friend Obed, thee has a little rebel beneath thy roof.

*Obed.* Nay, never heed her, Friend Bosworth. Her mother has an obstinate nature, and is apt to be a little tart of tongue; and the child is her constant companion. I grieve at this backsliding from the principles of our faith. But thee will find son Ephraim untainted with the war-spirit. He is a lad after my own heart. Come, let us go to my room. I would hear more of thy plans. (*Exit* L.)

*Bosworth* (*rises, sets back chair, turns, and looks at* RUTH). Verily, she is a little rebel. But when thee is mine, my pretty Ruth, I'll teach thee better. (*Exit* L.)

*Ruth* (*comes down* R.). I like not Friend Bosworth.

He looks no one in the face : he is soft of step, and hath a sneaking way of watching that troubles me. When my eyes are turned away, I can feel his eyes upon me, for a shudder, as though a snake was crossing my path, runs through me. He is not to be trusted. (*Enter* PRUDENCE *door in flat with pail and dipper.*)

*Prudence* (*comes* L.). Hallo, Miss Impudence, didn't I tell you not to come into the kitchen?

*Ruth.* Nay, thee must not be angry, Prudence. Father sent for me.

*Prudence.* Well, remember you are to touch nothing. Its no matter though, the washing's out. (*Knock at door*). Who's that? Come in. (*Enter* ELMER GRANGER *with gun : looks at* RUTH.)

*Elmer.* Is this the house of Obed Sterling? (*Sees* PRUDENCE : *drops gun.*) O Prudence, sister !

*Prudence.* Why, it's Elmer ! (*They run into each other's arms.*) Oh, I'm so glad to see you again !

*Elmer.* Why, sis, you dear little soul ! give us another buss.

*Prudence.* A dozen. Now, where did you come from, and what brings you here?

*Elmer.* I came here with our delegate to the convention from Massachusetts. Arrived at Philadelphia yesterday, saw a good day's work, had a good night's rest, and came out early this morning to hunt you up before I go back to witness the adoption of the declaration. Sis, the whole country is rising. It needs but that determined act to thrill all loyal hearts, and tyranny is crushed, our land is free. (*Looks at* RUTH, *who stands* R. *watching them.*) But there's somebody, Prudence. Manners, sis, manners. **2\***

*Prudence.* Why, that's Ruth. — Ruth, this is my brother Elmer.

*Elmer.* Hope you are well, marm.

*Ruth.* Nay, thee is mistaken, the mother is within: I am daughter Ruth.

*Prudence.* Ha, ha, ha! She's a funny little thing, Elmer.

*Elmer.* She's a beauty, sis. I'd like to shake hands with her.

*Prudence.* Then, why don't you? she won't bite.

*Ruth.* Thee is very welcome, Friend Elmer. I would like to shake hands with thee, but thee seem a bit bashful.

*Elmer.* Bashful! me? My gracious, sis, did you hear that?

*Prudence.* Ha, ha, ha! You're frightened, Elmer.

*Elmer* (*crossing to* RUTH). I am a rebel, Miss Ruth, in arms against a tyrant king. I would gladly give my life to see my country free. Will you give me your hand now?

*Ruth.* Yea, thee is a man after my own heart. Thee shall have both (*offers her hands, which he takes*). I love thy sister dearly : should I not share her pride in such a noble patriot as thee is?

*Elmer* (*pressing her hands*). Thank you. Sympathy for our cause from those whose principles forbid resistance, is a proof we are right. We only ask our liberty to hold what is our own, — nought else.

*Ruth.* Indeed! Yet thee now holds what is not thy own, — my hands.

*Elmer* (*dropping her hands*). I beg your pardon. I

— I —

*Ruth.* Nay, thee must not feel hurt: thee may have them again if 'twill please thee. (*Gives hands.*)

*Elmer.* Oh, you — (*drops them suddenly, and turns to* PRUDENCE). Sis, I must run, or I shall be in love with this fascinating little Quaker.

*Prudence.* Nonsense. Yankees never run. (*They talk together.*)

*Ruth* (*aside*). I never saw a man I liked so well. He hath a good form, a noble face, and eyes, ah! they make me shudder; not as Friend Bosworth's eyes do, but still a shudder, yet very pleasant to feel: I like it.

*Prudence.* I mustn't stop to talk with you now, Elmer: must get the washing things out of the way. You run into the garden with Ruth while I pick up a bit.

*Ruth.* Yea, Friend Elmer, I will show thee the way. Thee is not afraid to trust thyself with me?

*Elmer.* Afraid! (*aside*) but I am. (*Aloud.*) Oh, certainly not! will you take my arm?

*Ruth.* Nay, give me thy hand, and I will lead thee to the flower-beds. (*Gives hand, and leads him to door.*)

*Prudence.* Ah! Elmer? (*he turns*). Thee seems a bit bashful. Ha, ha, ha! (*He shakes his fist at her, then exit with* RUTH.) Well, he's provided for: so I'll go to work again. (*Goes behind tub, and dips water from tub to pail.*) It's just good to see that boy from the old place again. (*Enter* EPHRAIM, *door in* F., *quietly; stands at door a second, and looks at* PRUDENCE, *then creeps to door* R. U. E., *listens, then steps over to* PRUDENCE, *raises her face, and kisses her; then steps quickly back to door, and stands meekly twirling his thumbs, with eyes turned to the ceiling.*

*Prudence (as he kisses her).* Murder! thieves! (*Turns, and looks at* EPHRAIM.) Ephraim Sterling!

*Ephraim.* Yea, Friend Prudence, here I am once more.

*Prudence.* Yes, I felt your presence before you spoke. How dare you?

*Ephraim.* Verily I have travelled far this morning, my lips were parched with thirst: thine were like a tempting bunch of cherries, and I did fall into temptation. Art thou not glad I am at home again?

*Prudence (keeps at work bailing out her tub).* Yes, I'm glad when the cows are at home, the hens and chickens on their perch, and the pigs quietly asleep in their pens.

*Ephraim.* Cows, hens, hogs! Verily, Friend Prudence, thee takes me for a brute.

*Prudence.* No, indeed, for brutes will fight. Even a rat will defend himself when driven to a corner.

*Ephraim.* Thee knows my love of peace. Am I not a Friend?

*Prudence.* Fiddlesticks! Whose friend, when you have not the courage or the will to defend and protect the oppressed?

*Ephraim (attempts to take her hand).* Thee knows I would be more than a friend to thee, that I love thee. (*She resents his attempt to take her hand, and here slips a piece of soap into his hand. He looks at it, and throws it into the tub with a splash.*) What nonsense is this?

*Prudence.* You talk so fast, I thought you might be short of soap. Ha, ha, ha!

*Ephraim.* Be serious, Prudence. I would have thee be my wife.

*Prudence.* You! why, a man of peace can only be a piece of a man any way. I mean to have a whole one, or none; whole-hearted, whole-souled, with a bump of combativeness to match the bump of benevolence. The man to win a Yankee girl's heart must be as determined as the motto on the old flag, "Don't tread on me."

*Ephraim.* No man should tread on me.

*Prudence.* No, you would crawl out of his way.

*Ephraim.* Yea, I would remove myself from his path.

*Prudence.* How very kind! But suppose you should see one of those *brave* Tories, who take every opportunity to insult defenceless women, put his arm about my waist?

*Ephraim (fiercely).* I would knock him down.

*Prudence.* But that would be violence.

*Ephraim.* Thee is right. I would lay him gently on the earth, and sit quietly on his prostrate form till thee was out of sight.

*Prudence.* You would protect me?

*Ephraim.* With my life. Will thee not give me the right to protect thee?

*Prudence.* No, the man who wins me must help free my country.

*Ephraim.* Yea, I will be that man.

*Prudence.* You, a born Quaker?

*Ephraim.* I will be born again. Thy love shall make me strong, valiant, yea, for thy sake I will become a desperado. (*Strikes hand on tub.*)

*Prudence* Well, don't upset my tub, then. Ephraim, if I thought I could depend upon you, I would —

*Ephraim* (*eagerly*).   Yea, thee would —

*Prudence*.   Ask thee to help me with the tub.

*Ephraim*.   Nay, thee mocks me.   I'll have no more to say to thee.   (*Comes down* L.)

*Prudence*.   That's right, Ephraim.   Silence is so becoming to a Quaker!   (*Sings.*)

> Father and I went down to camp,
>     Along with Siah Baker;
> And there we saw the patriot boys,
>     But not a single Quaker.

(*Enter* GINGER *while she is singing, door in flat, and joins in chorus.*)

> Yankee Doodle, &c. (*as before*).

*Ephraim*.   Yea, the Friends may well call her a firebrand, for she'll drive me to the battle-field in spite of myself.   (*Exit* L.)

*Ginger*.   Dat's de camp-meeting for me.   When you gwine down dar again, Miss Prudence?

*Prudence*.   Here, Ginger, catch hold of the tub.

*Ginger*.   Yas, indeed.   (*They take tub from bench, and set it on stage near* L).   Hallo, who's dat?

(*Enter* RUTH *and* ELMER, *door in flat: he has his arm about her waist.*)

*Ruth*.   Thee sees I have brought thy brother back safe, Prudence.

*Elmer*.   And we've had a delightful ramble.

*Prudence*.   Yes, you have *waisted* no time in getting acquainted.   (RUTH *sits on settle.*)   Come, Ginger, take out the bench.

*Elmer.* Hallo, this is Ginger: I've heard of him.

*Prudence.* And Ginger has heard of you. — This is my brother Elmer, Ginger.

*Ginger.* By golly, you don't mean it! Massa Elmer, you's jes one ob de patriots. (*Bows and scrapes.*)

*Elmer.* Give me your hand, Ginger.

*Ginger.* Wh-wh-what! you gwine to shake hands wid a darky?

*Elmer* (*shaking hands*). Yes, and proud to have the chance, Ginger. My sister has told me how boldly you came to her rescue, when a Tory dared to step across her path. You're a brave fellow.

*Ginger.* Tank you, massa. (*Holds up his hand.*) Ole hand, you's been shook by a brave man: dar sha'n't no more soap and water wipe out dat are honor, chile, neber. By golly, dese Down-Easters be white men; day'll be freeing all de darkies one ob dese days. (*Takes up bench, and goes to door.*) Tank you, Massa Elmer. I's a poor old darky, but I got a heart, and, if I could die for you and Miss Prudence, I'd do it freely. (*Exit door* F.)

*Elmer.* Now, Prudence, come and sit down: I've much to say to you.

*Prudence.* No: work first, and pleasure afterwards. (*Takes up pail.*) I must go for water.

*Elmer* (*taking pail*). Not while I am here: where shall I find it?

*Prudence.* I'll show you, come. (*Exit* PRUDENCE *and* ELMER, *door in flat.*)

*Ruth.* I like Friend Elmer. What a pity he's one

of the world's people! But yet I think I like him
the better for that. None of the Friends can talk so
sweetly and so bravely. (*Enter* L. *Bosworth.*)

*Bosworth* (*aside*). I have found her alone at last.
Friend Obed seems to be of a wavering nature. I fear
I cannot depend much upon his assistance. I'll know
my fate here at once. (*Aside.*) Friend Ruth.

*Ruth.* Well, Friend Bosworth.

*Bosworth.* I have told thy father that I love thee.

*Ruth.* Indeed! Thee never told me as much.

*Bosworth.* I tell thee now, that I love thee dearly.

*Ruth.* Has thee seen the young patriot, Elmer·
Granger?

*Bosworth.* Thee does not mean to tell me the brother
of Prudence is here?

*Ruth.* Yea, he is here. We have held sweet con-
verse together, and I like him. He is so comely and
brave, I think he would inspire thee with admiration,
Friend Bosworth, and thee is not a man easily moved.

*Bosworth.* We will speak of him another time. I
told thee that I loved thee.

*Ruth.* I heard thee, and thought how pleasant would
be those words from the lips of Friend Elmer.

*Bosworth.* Ruth Sterling, would thee insult me?
Does thee not know that this language indicates a
marked preference for this young rebel?

*Ruth.* Nay, I did not know it; but, if thee thinks it
does, I'm very glad.

*Bosworth.* Ruth Sterling, thee must think of him no
more. It is thy father's wish that thee shall become
my wife. Ruth, Ruth, thee knows not how dearly I

love thee.  (*Sits beside her, and attempts to take her hand: she rises indignantly.*)

*Ruth.*  Be silent, I command thee; not even my father's wish shall compel me to hear such words from thy lips.

*Bosworth.*  Be warned in time, Ruth.  Thy father's life is in my hands.  Consent to be my wife, and in the coming struggle I will protect him; refuse, and I give him up to the ruthless hands of the advancing foe.

*Ruth.*  Thee speaks falsely, Uriel Bosworth.  My father can owe nothing to thee, and if he did would rather die than peril his daughter's happiness.  Begone!

*Bosworth.*  Nay, Ruth (*puts his arm about her waist, and seizes her hand*).  I'll not be repulsed so coolly.

*Ruth* (*struggling*).  Release me, I command thee.

*Bosworth.*  I will be heard.  (*Enter* ELMER, *door in flat, with pail; drops it; seizes* BOSWORTH, *and hurls him across stage.*)

*Elmer.*  You have been heard, friend.  (*Enter* MRS. STERLING, R. 1 E.; OBED *and* EPHRAIM, L.)  You see you have aroused the whole family.

*Obed.*  Daughter Ruth, I heard thy voice raised in anger.

*Bosworth.*  Friend Obed, I am to blame.  Carried away by the love which thee knows burns within me, I urged my suit so warmly as to frighten Ruth.  She must pardon and forget.

*Ruth.*  Yea, Friend Bosworth.  I will pardon, but I cannot forget.

3

*Obed.* Stranger, thee is welcome.

*Ruth.* He is no stranger, father. This is Elmer Granger.

*Obed.* The brother of Prudence? Thee is heartily welcome. (*Gives his hand.*)

*Elmer.* Thanks, Friend Sterling. (*Enter* PRUDENCE *door in* F.)

*Prudence.* Yes, that's my big brother. Come, Ephraim, you should know him.

*Ephraim.* Friend Elmer, I am glad to meet thee. (*Shakes hands.*)

*Elmer.* I've heard of you. Prudence often writes. I think you've a warm corner in her heart.

*Prudence* (*pinching him*). You silly goose! You'll spoil every thing.

*Elmer.* Then I'll be dumb as an oyster.

(ELMER C.; PRUDENCE R. C.; RUTH *on settle;* MRS. S. *stands behind her, with hand on her shoulder;* OBED L. C.; EPHRAIM *next* L.; *and* BOSWORTH *extreme left.*)

*Obed.* Thee has seen stormy times in thy native place; thee has suffered deeply in this wicked rebellion.

*Elmer.* Wicked rebellion? You are wrong, friend. If ever the torch of war is lighted in a holy cause, 'tis when it flames above the altar of liberty. Remember that 'twas only after the iron heel of the oppressor had trampled on our hard-won harvest that we rose defiant. I have seen the home of my childhood laid in ashes, my father shot down by foreign hirelings who had no rights to enforce, no homes to protect, our dearest rights insulted to feed the vanity of the despot who sits on England's throne. He would be a coward in-

deed, who, with such blighting wrongs to avenge, would
not dare all to free the land of such a curse.

*Bosworth.* Young blood is hot, and fiery words but
cheap. Save thy breath : *we* are loyal to Friend George.

*Mrs. S.* (*coming down*). Nay, speak for thyself,
Friend Bosworth. — Friend Elmer, thee is welcome.
(*Gives her hand.*) Thee sees they have forgotten
me : I am Rachel Sterling.

*Elmer* (*clasping her hand*). My dear mother's true
and steadfast friend.

*Mrs. S.* Yea, it was a sore trial to my friendship
when she left us to mate with one of the world's people.

*Elmer.* But you were true to her always. You
showed your love by giving my sister a home. Poor
mother, hers was a hard fate. I could not sorrow for my
father ; for he died bravely, with musket in hand. But
mother — curse the fiend that basely struck her down !
They told me that our home was in flames. I left the
ranks of the little band, who were struggling against
the foe, and rushed home to protect my mother. As I
neared the house I saw her flying from its door, pursued
by one Richard Cross, a renegade, who had led our
foes to plunder. Even as I looked he raised the sword
he bore, and struck her down. I flew at him, seized
his weapon, and struck at his bared head. He raised
his hand, and caught the blow, then turned and fled. I
could not overtake him, and returned to meet a last
look from my mother's eyes, as she sunk in death,
The renegade fled from our town. He bears the mark
of the sword on his right hand ; and, should we ever

meet, my mother's death shall be terribly avenged. (BOSWORTH *hides his right hand in his bosom.*)

*Mrs. S.* Nay, thee must not speak of vengeance; let the man of sin depart in peace; within he bears his punishment. Thy mother was a good woman. I am glad she wed the man of her choice.

*Elmer.* Then you have not the Friends' prejudice against marriage outside the sect.

*Mrs. S.* I may have the prejudice; but I would not stand in the way of happiness.

*Elmer.* Even were it your own daughter?

*Mrs. S.* Yea. My daughter Ruth shall make her choice; and I shall love him even though he be of the world's people.

*Prudence* (*aside to* ELMER). Hear that, brother. Don't lose the opportunity. Ruth may be yours.

*Elmer* (*aside to* PRUDENCE). I'll win the little Quaker, in spite of the scowling Friend yonder. (*Enter* GINGER, *door in* F.)

*Ginger.* Here comes old Pretzel, running like de debble. Somefin's broke, sure for sartin.

*Prudence.* Well, you break for that teakettle. I must scald out my tub.

*Ginger* (*goes to fireplace*). I'll fotch him, Miss Prudence.

(*Enter* PRETZEL, *door in flat, with his hand to his nose, which is bleeding.*)

*Pretzel.* Murter, tieves! Mine prains is broke, ant my heat all running avay. Look at dot, see de bleet dot I ish shedding for mine country.

*Obed.* What's the trouble, friend Pretzel?

*Pretzel.*  De Tories come to mine house.  Dey proke mine vindows, dey lets mine peer all runt avay, ant dey vill pull der house up to der grount if somepody don't come right avay pretty quick.

*Elmer.*  The dastard.  Another outrage to rouse the slumbering patriotism of your insulted people!  They shall find one strong arm to bar the way.

*Pretzel.*  Dot's right.  You're a prave young man.  Dey vill run vhen dey see you.  Go right avay quick, ant I vill vait here till you come pack.  (*Going* L.)

*Elmer.*  No, you must lead the way.  Come, come: we lose time.  (*Takes his gun.*)  Now, friends, we have an opportunity to show these cowards what a few brave men can do.  Who will follow?  (*All stand silent.*)  Must I be alone in this good work?

*Bosworth.*  We are a peaceable people, we meddle not with broils.  Thee will find none here to assist thee.

*Elmer.*  Indeed, I expected little from you.  You have the air of a coward, one who would force his love upon an unwilling woman.  You need not scowl.  I fear you not.

*Prudence.*  Oh, I wish I was a man!  Bring me that kettle, Ginger.

*Ginger* (*brings kettle over to tub*).  Yas, indeed, and den I'm wid you, Massa Elmer.

*Prudence* (*pours boiling water into tub.*  GINGER *stands just* L. *of tub*).  I'd like to scald somebody.  Might make a little stir.  Lord knows there's some needed here.

*Elmer.*  Ginger, you're a brave fellow: come, we've

3*

no time to lose. — Hear me, friends. I know not the number of the foe. For myself I care not, but I would have our onset a success. Remember, if this outrage is not quickly avenged, you may be the next victims. For your own sakes be wise. Come (*pause*). Shame! In a neighbor's cause will not one join with us to prevent outrage?

*Obed.* Nay: our faith forbids violence. Not one.

*Ephraim* (*stepping to* c.). Yea, there is one: I will join thee.

*Obed, Bosworth, Ruth.* Thee!

*Ephraim.* Yea, I. There's my hand, Friend Elmer. Tell me what to do, where to strike, and thee will find the Quaker's arm is strong for the right. (*Prudence goes off*, L.)

*Obed.* Son Ephraim! Is thee gone mad? thee will disgrace the coat of drab.

*Ephraim* (*taking off his coat, and throwing it down*). Nay, I'll leave it behind. 'Twill give me more freedom. I will smite the enemy with my fists. If I only had a gun now! (*Enter Prudence*, L.)

*Prudence.* Here it is, Ephraim. I brought it from Concord, that I might give it to the brave man who would fight for me. O Ephraim! (*Throws her arms about his neck, and kisses him.*)

*Ephraim.* Verily, I wax strong for the fight. On, Friend Elmer, on!

*Ginger.* Golly, dar's fight in de young Quaker.

*Elmer* (*gives his hand to Ephraim*). Thanks, you are a good true man, a friend indeed.

*Bosworth.* You'll repent this, young man.

*Elmer.* Silence. Dare you stand between a man and his country's cause? Young blood is hot, and fiery words are cheap, you say. My deeds shall speak for me. — Come, Pretzel.

*Pretzel.* Yaw. I vill pe mit you pretty quick. (*Passes* GINGER, *and steps on his toe.*)

*Ginger.* Ow, dat ar corn again! (*Pushing* PRETZEL, *he sits down in tub of water.*)

*Pretzel* (*with hands on sides of tub raises himself*). Py gracious, someting's purning!

*Ginger.* Yah, yah, yah! dat Dutchman always in hot water.

TABLEAU. — ELMER *and* EPHRAIM *at door with hands clasped;* PRUDENCE L. *back;* PRETZEL *in tub;* GINGER *next* L., *laughing;* BOSWORTH *extreme* L.; RUTH *stands by fireplace with hands clasped, looking intently at* EL- MER; MRS. STERLING *behind settle watching* EPHRAIM; OBED R. *Curtain.*

*From the time of Pretzel's entrance, let the speech be quick, the action rapid.*

Act II. *Evening. Scene same as in Act I. Curtain at window drawn. Bright fire in fireplace.
Candle burning on table.* PRUDENCE *seated at table
sewing, or spinning if there is a wheel on stage.*
MRS. STERLING *on settle knitting.* OBED *seated in a
chair, which is set back against scene* R., *near fireplace
next* 1 E.; *his head leaning back, with a silk handkerchief thrown over it; his hands folded across his
breast.*

*Prudence.* After a storm comes a calm. The ven-
erable Obed and his spouse have been having what
would be called among the world's people, a spat. I
never heard two people go on so; and now he's evi-
dently disciplining himself for rebelling against the
spirit of peace. (OBED *groans.*) No, he's waking up
again.

*Obed (snatching off handkerchief).* I tell thee,
Rachel, thee is a foolish woman. Thee has listened
to the mutterings of the rebellious; thee has given
thy heart; yea, encouraged thy daughter to sympathize
with the discontented, and now our own children turn
against us.

*Mrs. S.* Speak for thyself, Obed. Our children
have not turned against *me*, and I blame not myself that
they have a warm interest in the success of the right.

*Obed (groans).* Yea, verily, peace hath fled from our
dwelling. This firebrand cometh among us with his
warlike tongue, and our daughter warmeth towards

him ; and our son forsaketh the path of peace, and goeth forth to slay.  It shall not be.  The girl shall be locked in her chamber, and the boy —

*Mrs. S.*   Nay.  Be not a fool, Obed.  Thee might as well attempt to stop the whirlwind as to quench the fire of patriotism when 'tis kindled in a man's breast, or to smother love when once it hath found a resting-place in a maiden's heart.

*Prudence (aside).*  That's what I call sound doctrine.

*Obed.*  Rachel, thee is mad.  Knows thee not that the fruitage of love is marriage, and Friends cannot marry out of their own sect?

*Mrs. S.*   Thee knows 'tis a clause in our creed to which I could never give approval.  Does thee remember Hester Page, who loved the father of Elmer and Prudence?  She was beloved by all.  She married, and the Friends turned from her.  I felt they were unjust to her ; that she deserved better treatment after all her devotion to the good works among us.  She fell a martyr in the cause of liberty ; and if I could atone for our neglect of her by the gift of our daughter to her son, — her noble son, — I would consent, though all the Friends with uplifted hands and looks of horror should cry, "Nay."

*Prudence (aside).*  Glory hallelujah !

*Obed.*  Nay, be silent : thee'll get a smart talking-to at the next Yearly Meeting.

*Mrs. S.*   Yea ; but I have a tongue, and can talk back, Obed.

*Obed.*  Yea, and drown the elders with thy clamor.

*Ginger* (*outside*).   Bress de Lord, I'se home! Hallo
Massa Eph., is yer comin'?   (*Enter door in* F.)

*Prudence* (*rising*).   Why, Ginger, where have you
been all day?   Where's Ephraim and Elmer?   Is any-
body hurt?   Why don't you speak?

*Ginger*.   Now, jes you hole on, Miss Prudence.
Does yer tink I's gwine to answer forty-leben ques-
tions widout a breaf?   Here I is: dat's nuff for me.

*Mrs. S.*   Are the lads safe, Ginger?

*Ginger*.   Wa'l, I dunno, misses.   I'm safe, an'
dat's de most consequential.   I'll tole you all about
it.   We went down dar to old Pretzel's dis mornin',
Massa Elmer, Massa Eph., an' — an' Ginger, dat's
me.   De old Dutchman, he's a sneak; he jis watch his
chance, and when we wasn't looking he clared, he did.
But we went down dar, got mos' to de house, and we
hear de wus yellin' dat eber was.   Den Massa Elmer,
he says, says he, Hole on, let's squirmish a bit: so
we lay down onto de grass and squirmished up to de
fence; den worked on up to de woodpile, and made
dat a sort of a-a-a bull-whack.   Den Massa Elmer
and Massa Eph. dey loaded der muskats, an' I loaded
a big stick off de woodpile.   Dat ar Massa Eph., by
golly, I nebber seed a man so nerbous in my life; he
kept a pourin' in de powder an' de shot, and ram-
ing down, till he must have had six bustin' charges in
dat ar muskat.   Den we looked round de corner ob de
woodpile, an' dar was six Tory fellows a-sittin' on de
grass, wid a keg of old Pretzel's beer an'-an' sour
kruet, an'-an'-snasengers, jes a stuffin' an' drinkin'.
Den Massa Elmer sings out, Blaze away, boys, an'-an'

let fly.  Den Massa Eph., he sings out, an' he let fly.
Dar was an explosion like a cannon: de old muskat
kicked; an' Massa Eph., he jes layed on his back an'
hollered.  But dem are Tories dey jes scooted down
the road, wid Massa Elmer an' Massa Eph. loading
up and blazin' away.  Dey dropped four on 'em.  We
kep' up de chase three hours;. den we lost sight of
Massa Elmer an' de Tories, and turned back.

*Prudence.*  Did you forsake Elmer?

*Ginger.*  No, chile, he forsake us.  Couldn't keep
up wid him no how.

*Mrs. S.*  But where's Ephraim?

*Eph.*  (*Enter door in* F.)  Yea, verily, he is here.

(*His coat and vest are gone, one of his stockings is
hanging over his shoe, the sleeve of his shirt is ripped up,
elbow scraped, a red handkerchief round his head, one
eye blacked, and face begrimed with powder and dust,
gun in hand.*)

*Obed* (*groans*).  Ephraim, my son, does thee return
to us in such a pitiful plight?

*Ephraim.*  Yea, I have smelt the smoke of battle,
I have smitten the despoiler with snipe-shot.  I have felt
the butt of my musket in near proximity to my eye.  I
have sat in the dust, and, in the language of the world's
people, have had a jolly good fight.

*Ginger.*  Dat's so; and won de victory.

*Obed* (*groans*).  Ephraim, my son, my heart is
sore troubled.  Thee was reared a child of peace;
thee is now a man of war and sin; thee has brought
shame to our house.

*Ephraim* (*boldly*).  Nay, father, I have brought no

shame. What right have I, with all the blood and sinews of a man, to sit idly down and talk of peace, when my countrymen east, west, north, and south, are roused to arms, at the encroaching of tyranny upon their rights and liberties? I have been reared a child of peace, and the inward spirit now teaches me there shall be no peace until we, with brave, stout hearts and strong right arms, have taught the intruders we have the power to maintain it. (*Comes down* L.)

*Prudence* (*clapping her hands*). Hurray! Them's my sentiments.

*Mrs. S.* Prudence, thee forgets thyself. — Ephraim, my son, thy person needs proper care.

*Ephraim.* Yea; and I am as hungry as the bear that roameth the wilderness. (*Enter* BOSWORTH, *door in flat.*)

*Bosworth.* Ah, Ephraim has returned. What transformations here, child of Belial?

*Ephraim* (*stepping forward quickly*). Nay, Friend Bosworth, thee had better keep a civil tongue in thy head. The fires of war are yet hot within me, and peradventure thy skull may open wider than thy mouth.

*Bosworth.* Dares thee threaten me?

*Ephraim.* Yea, I dare, for thee is a smooth, sneaking traitor, Friend Bosworth. (*Advancing on him.*)

*Obed* (*stepping before* BOSWORTH). Stand back, Ephraim : in my house a guest is sacred.

*Prudence.* Land sakes! I never saw a man so full of fight.

*Ginger.* Yaas. I guess dar ain't much stuffin' in his buzzum.

*Obed.* Go to thy room, Ephraim. When thee is thyself, I'll speak with thee.

*Mrs. S.* Come, Ephraim, thy mother will attend thee. (*Pats him upon the shoulder.*) Thee is fiery, but 'tis in a good cause, and thy mother is proud of thee. (*Exeunt* Mrs. S. *and* EPHRAIM, L.)

*Ginger.* Miss Prudence, can't you find me somfin to gnaw? ain't tasted noffin since breakfus.

*Prudence (coming to* R. U. E.) Yes, come with me: I can find a cold fowl. (*Exit.*)

*Ginger (following).* Dat's good, jes let me get foul of it, and gib it a burial-place.

*Bosworth.* Friend Obed, I grieve with thee, that the child of thy faith should have gone the way of wickedness.

*Obed.* Thee needn't trouble thyself, Friend Bosworth. Thee has sins enough of thine own to grieve for. The lad's spirit has been aroused, he hath found he has a strong arm, that his country needs him. If he must fight, I hope his aim will be sure, and the enemy bite the dust before him.

*Bosworth.* Obed Sterling, is *thee* turning traitor too? Beware! thee is a marked man. Give these rebels sympathy even in thy thoughts, and nought can save thee.

*Obed.* Hark thee, Friend Bosworth : thee has dared to threaten me before. I have borne with thee because thee has been our friend (*fiercely*) ; but, if thee dare use such words to me again, I will pitch thee out of yonder window.

*Bosworth (aside).* The old man is stubborn. I

4

must dissemble. (*Aloud.*) Nay, nay! Friend Obed. I meant not to threaten; I would but point out to thee thy danger. Thee shall have all protection from me. Verily it would be base in me to persecute thee, when I love thy daughter so dearly.

*Obed.* Thee has spoken with my daughter?

*Bosworth.* Yea, I did urge my suit, but was interrupted by that wicked wretch, Elmer Granger. Beware of him. He looks upon the girl with favor. There is danger in his presence. Secure thy daughter's safety by giving me thy promise she shall be mine.

*Obed.* I told thee I would sleep upon it. As thee seems in haste, we will settle the matter now. Here comes my daughter. (*Enter* RUTH 1 E. R.) Ruth, child, come hither. Thee sees Friend Bosworth, a man of strong build, and not uncomely, of good report among the Friends; not burdened with wealth, but active in its pursuit. He asks me to give him thy hand, would have thee be his wife.

*Bosworth.* Yea, Ruth, I love thee with my whole soul.

*Obed.* Speak, daughter: thy fate is in thy own hands. Neither thy father nor thy mother will prevent thy free choice.

*Ruth.* Father, thee has ever been kind to me. Never an unkind word has thee given me. From my earliest days thee has been ever watchful over my thoughts and wishes. No blessing thee could bestow has ever been withheld. I honor thee above all men. Thy judgment is so wise that thy word is law to me. I know Friend Bosworth professes love for me;

and yet my heart has felt no answering thrill to his protestations. I shrink from his glance, and tremble in his presence. Nay, I will be frank. Another, with no words, with no entreaties, has touched a chord within my being that vibrates with ecstasy at his approach. He is of the world's people, yet brave, strong, and true. Yet I am but a child, and may not know my own heart. My fate I leave in thy hands. Speak, father: what thee says shall guide me.

*Obed (takes* RUTH's *hand, kisses her on the forehead, then turns to* BOSWORTH). Friend Bosworth, thee has thy answer. (*Comes to* L.)

*Bosworth* (C.). Nay, this will not serve. I must have a plain answer, yes, or no.

*Obed (sternly)*. No. A thousand times no. My daughter is not for such as thou.

*Bosworth.* Nay, bear with me, Friend Obed.

*Obed.* Nay, thy friend no more, Bosworth. I have borne with thee until Patience is indignant at me. By thy own confession, thee is a spy; but that I feared my daughter loved thee, I would have driven thee from my house, when thee first spoke. Now, I tell thee, quit my house.

*Bosworth.* Has thee forgotten I can destroy thee?

*Obed.* Do thy worst. No harm can come to him who obeys the voice of conscience.

*Bosworth.* Then, dread my vengeance. You know me not. You thought I was a cowardly Quaker. I have deceived you and your tribe. The opinions of your sect are known to me; ay, and all their wealth, and where 'tis to be found. One motive only has kept me in

your midst, — love for your daughter. She scorns me.
Now comes my turn. I will seize, burn, destroy, till
you shall tremble at my name (*goes to door*). You have
need of all your caution. The hour of vengeance is
approaching. Ruth Sterling, you tremble in my presence: ha, ha, ha! Present or absent, you shall now
tremble at the thought of me, for I swear you shall
be mine. (*Exit door in flat.*)

*Ruth* (*running to* OBED: *they meet in* C. *of stage*).
O father, father! he terrifies me.

*Obed.* Nay, fear not, child, He is a bad, wicked
man; but he cannot harm thee. Go to thy rest.
(*Leads her to* 1 E. R.)

*Ruth.* But, father, thee is grieved that I love Elmer
Granger.

*Obed* (*groans*). He is of the world's people. The
Friends will groan in spirit; but thee has said, no blessing I could bestow upon thee was ever withheld. Go to
thy rest in peace. (*Exit Ruth* 1 E. R.)

*Obed* (*groans*). Verily, Friend Obed, thee is running up a long account for settlement at Yearly Meeting. (*Enter* EPHRAIM *from door* L.; *costume same
as in Act I., spruce and clean, gun in his hand.*)
Ephraim, my son, thee is not going out on the war-
path again?

*Eph.* Yea, father. Friend Elmer may need my help.
I go to seek him.

*Obed.* Give me thy hand, Ephraim. (*They shake
hands.*) It grieves me that thee is become a man of
war; but, if thee must go, remember the maxim of the
world's people, "Put thy trust in Providence, and keep

thy powder dry.'' And do not forget the words of that brave but sinful Friend, Israel Putnam, " Wait until thee sees the white of their eyes." Peace go with thee, my son !

*Eph* ( *patting gun*). Yea, I have it in my hands.

*Obed* (*groans*). Yea, Rachel is right; but the women must not have it all their own way. (*Exit* L. 1 E.)

*Eph.* Now I will seek Friend Elmer. (*Goes up. Enter* PRUDENCE, *door* R. U. E.)

*Prudence.* Ephraim, you are not going out again to-night?

*Eph.* Verily, Friend Prudence, it is not right that I should leave thy brother in the midst of wolves. I go to seek him.

*Prudence.* O Ephraim ! you a perfect fire-eater, — a man that I am proud to call my lover.

*Eph.* Nay, thee is mistaken. I am no woman's lover.

*Prudence.* What? Didn't you make love to me over the washing this morning?

*Eph.* Yea, I did speak some tender words of non-sense in thine ear.

*Prudence.* In my ear ! Why, you kissed me !

*Eph.* Yea, I did imprint the seal of friendship upon thy lips. But I have another mistress now.

*Prudence.* You don't mean to say you've fallen in love with another woman ! Who is she?

*Eph.* My country. Thee did mock my profession of peace. Thee did call me a coward. And I girded on my armor, and went forth to battle.

4*

*Prudence.* Yes, I aroused the manhood within you, and made you a patriot.

*Eph.* Yea, and so filled my heart with martial fire, it hath not room for any tenderer flame. If thee loves me, thee is to be pitied, for thee has given me to another and a sterner mistress. The war-drum rings in my ears, the flash of musketry is before my eyes. I I hunger for the fight, and have no appetite for love. Fare thee well, Friend Prudence. If thee has lost a lover, thy country has found a defender. (*Sings.*)

> Yankee Doodle, keep it up,
> Yankee Doodle dandee;
> Mind the music and the steps,
> And leave the girls behind thee.

[*Exit door in F.*

*Prudence.* Well, I never! Mittened by a Quaker! I shall never hold up my head again. I've roused the lion, and lost the lamb; the Quaker wasn't worth having, but the soldier's quite another article. Oh dear, dear, dear! this comes of meddling with politics. Maybe he'll get shot, and I'll have his death to answer for. Ah Prudence! I'm afraid you care more for this fellow than you dream of. (*Takes up candle.*) I'm not going to lose any sleep for him. (*Crosses to* R. 1 E.) He hungers for the fight. Ah Ephraim! courage may serve you in the battle, but Prudence is a virtue not to be despised. (*Exit* 1 E.)

(*Enter* GINGER R. U. E., *gnawing a bone.*)

*Ginger.* Dah, dat ar fowl's gone to roost. I've cleaned the cubburd of all de eatables and drinkables.

Dunno what dey'll do for breakfus in de mornin, but de clams ob hunger must be dissatisfied if it breeds a famine. Eberybody gone to bed, den I'll go out to de barn and snooze myself. Hallo, what dat? (*Listens at door.*) Sh! dar's sumbody prowlin 'round de house. Whispers. Halt, Ginger, das mischif in de wind. Keep dark, honey. (*Lies down behind settle. Door is pushed open slowly, and* BOSWORTH *looks in, then creeps cautiously down, listens at door* L., *then goes back to door in flat, and beckons.*)

(*Enter* BURKE *and* BLUCHER, *with guns.* All three come down stage, BURKE R., BLUCHER L., BOSWORTH C.)

*Burke.* Look here, Broadbrim. What kind of a job is this?

*Blucher.* Yes. Plunder, or murder? Speak out.

*Bosworth.* Silence! (*Creeps to door,* L., *and turns key.*) There, I've locked in the only one from whom we might expect interruption, — young Sterling. He's had a fight to-day, so he'll sleep soundly now.

*Blucher.* We can easily give him a sleeping-powder, if you say the words (*slapping gun*).

*Blucher.* With a pill added that will be sure to quiet him.

*Bosworth.* Hist! What brings you here to-night?

*Burke.* It's all along of that fight at the Dutchman's this morning. We were surprised by an infernal rebel, who drove us beyond Carter's, until his comrades deserted; and then we turned and took him. I wanted to swing him to a tree, but the cap'n said no; he was a brave fellow, and we must take him down to camp, and honor him with a shooting.   So we took him down there, tied him to a tree, and went to supper.   When supper was gone, we found the rebel gone also.   So Blue and I were detailed to retake him. We tracked him to within a mile of this house, and then lost him.

*Bosworth.*   But you are on his track now.   He and the owner of this place, Obed Sterling, are leagued together.

*Blucher.*   Sterling !   Why, Sterling's a Quaker.

*Bosworth.*   He's a traitor.   You know me?

*Burke.*   Know you, Broadbrim, the spy?   Ay, we have orders from Cap'n Trot to obey you when the service requires.

*Bosworth.*   Ay, I have need of you now.   My orders from headquarters are to shoot this Sterling ; to seize his daughter, and take her to Carter's.

*Blucher.*   Oh, we don't want to meddle with girls !

*Bosworth.*   The service demands obedience.

*Blucher.*   All right, Broadbrim.

*Bosworth.*   Then you look out for the old man, and I'll take care of the girl.   First to arouse Sterling. You, Blucher, go beneath the window of his room, at that corner (*points to* L. 1 E.), throw up a stone ; he'll open the window ; tell him Friend Garner is sick and needs him ; that will bring him out.   When he appears make short work of him, for he is a traitor to the king, and well  deserves what  he  must  receive, — instant death.

*Burke.*   Never fear.   I seldom lose a shot.

*Blucher.*   Nor I.   Old Deadeye is sure death.

*Bosworth.* Be cautious. Give me ten minutes to secure the girl, then follow my instructions.

*Blucher,* All right. But who pays the funeral expenses?

*Bosworth (handing him a purse).* The King of England.

*Blucher (throws up purse).* Long live the king!

*Bosworth.* Now away. Hush! who's that? (*Enter* PRETZEL, *door in flat.* BLUCHER *and* BURKE *crouch on the floor* R. *and* L.)

*Pretzel.* Ha, ha! Friend Sterling; wash you op? Dot is goot. I ish as try as never vas. Dose rascals trink op all mine peer, and I coome to get some of your cider. Hy! vhat is dot? Friend Sterling, you is not Friend Sterling after all.

*Ginger (peeps over settle).* By golly, dat ar Dutchman in anoder scrape.

*Bosworth.* What do you want here?

*Pretzel (shaking).* Oh, notings if you bleese. I just got run ober from mine house. Didn't know you had gompany. (BURKE *and* BLUCHER *rise, and point guns at him.*) Mine gracious gootness, ton't you do dot (*falls on his knees*). I'm only a poor Tuchman vidout fader or moder.

*Bosworth.* Get up, fool.

*Pretzel.* Yaw, right avay puty quick (*rises*). Ef you bleese, don't explode your guns mit me. I'm ony a poor —

*Bosworth.* Shut up!

*Pretzel.* Yaw. I like to say notings mit my mout shut.

*Bosworth.* Take him out and lock him in the barn.

*Pretzel.* In ter parn mit ter pigs? I don't like dot puty vell.

*Bosworth.* Do as I bid you; if he opens his mouth, throw him in the horse-pond.

*Pretzel.* Dot's vhat you call horspuddality. I don't like dot.

*Blucher.* Come, start, Dutchy.

*Pretzel.* Yaw, don't pint dem tings; dey might go off.

*Burke.* After you. (PRETZEL *backs up to door.* BURKE *and* BLUCHER *follow with their guns pointed at him.*)

*Pretzel.* Dis is too pad. You don't got some pizness here, an' I don't got mine cider. (*They threaten him with guns; he exits in a hurry, followed by* BLUCHER *and* BURKE.)

*Bosworth.* Now, then, my pretty Ruth, if you won't be mine by fair means, you shall by foul. (*Creeps slowly to* R. 1. E.)

*Ginger* (*rises*). Der's gwine to be trouble in dis yer family; it's about time I looked up Massa Eph. (*Exit door in* F.)

*Bosworth* (*turning quickly*). What's that? I thought I heard a step. It must have been Blucher (*turns to* R.). Ah, the pretty Ruth comes this way. 'Twill save the trouble of calling her. (*Creeps behind settle, and hides. Enter* RUTH *with a lighted candle: she places it on the table and goes to window, speaking as she enters.*)

*Ruth.* I cannot go to rest while Friend Elmer is in

danger.  If he is safe, he would have returned to see
his sister.  (*Looks .out of window.*)  Nay, 'tis very
dark.  What can have become of him!  He is brave
and noble, and his must be a good heart, it moves so
quickly at the call of distress.  I doubt if he thinks
of me.  Why should he?  Ah, that's a wise question,
too profound from my head, so I'll leave the heart to
answer it.  And that says yea, as there's truth in
his bright eyes, he does.  I wish he'd come.  His sister
must be so anxious about him, and she sleeps soundly.
I looked in upon her : she had thrown herself dressed
upon the bed and slept.  I could not do that, and yet
I am so anxious!  (BOSWORTH *rises.*)  Ah, who's that?
(*Comes down* L.)

*Bosworth* (*coming down* R.)  One not unknown to
you.

*Ruth.*  Thee here again!

*Bosworth.*  Ay, my pretty Ruth.  I could not leave
the Quaker fold and go out among the world's people
alone, and so I have returned for thee to bear me
company.

*Ruth.*  Thee does but jest, Uriel Bosworth, and
thy humor is so grim I like it not.

*Bosworth.*  No, it makes you tremble, pretty Ruth.
Come, you must go with me.  I told you you were
very dear to me.  I can't live without you.  You
have kindled .a fierce passion in my breast, — so fierce
that, were a thousand in my path, I'd slay them all
before I'd lose you.

*Ruth.*  Thee has no right to enter here.  Thee is
a base, bad man, sneaking like a thief, when darkness

covers the earth, into the house of the man thee *dares* not face in open daylight.

*Bosworth.*   I dare face thee, Ruth —

*Ruth.*   Ay, with a bold front but a coward heart. Thee is a traitor to our faith, a traitor to the cause of liberty, and, still greater shame, a traitor to the name of manhood.   Get thee hence!

*Bosworth.*   Ho, ho! bravely spoken, Ruth. You are a girl of spirit. You are a prize worth winning. But you forget you are alone and unprotected. Your brother is securely bound, your father doomed if he moves from his chamber.   I come not alone.

*Ruth.*   Thee is a brave man, Uriel Bosworth. Thy tyrant master must be proud of his followers who war upon women.

*Bosworth.*   Ruth Sterling, I swear —

*Ruth.*   Silence! Insult not my father's roof with an oath. Insult not his daughter with the profanation of that holy virtue which exists alone in honest hearts. Begone!

*Bosworth.*   Not without you, Ruth. You must go with me. Do not compel me to use force. You are unprotected.

*Ruth.*   Stand back, traitor. My protection is there (*points up*), though dangers surround me, He will securely guard and guide. Stand back, and let me pass.   (*Goes towards* R.)

*Bosworth* (*seizing her wrist*).   Nay, nay, my pretty Quaker. There is no escape. You must come with me.

*Ruth.*   Uriel Bosworth, release me.   (*Flinging off his hand, and going* L.)

*Bosworth* (*comes* R.) You cannot pass to your chamber. Hereafter the path of life we travel together. Come.

*Ruth.* Never. Thee has my father in thy power. I'll trust my fate to the darkness of the night. (*Runs up to door in flat.*)

*Bosworth* (*seizing her in* C. *of stage*). No, no, Ruth; trust to the light of my love.

*Ruth* (*struggling to free herself*). No, no! Rather death. Father! brother! Elmer, Elmer! (*Enter* ELMER *door in* R.)

*Elmer.* Here at thy call, Ruth (*strikes* BOSWORTH *a blow in his breast with his fist. He staggers back and falls* R. RUTH, *with a cry, throws herself upon* ELMER'S *breast*). Lie there, dog! — Nay, nay, do not tremble, Ruth: there is no danger.

*Bosworth* (*springing to his feet*). You lie, you cursed rebel! The house is surrounded by my friends. There is danger to you. Your fate is sealed. Release that girl!

*Elmer* (*quietly*). Certainly, if she desires it.

*Ruth* (*clinging to him*). Nay, nay, Friend Elmer.

*Elmer* (*with his arms about her*). You see she is contented here. (*Cooly.*) And I rather like it, Friend Bosworth.

*Bosworth.* I'll tear her from thee. (*Rushing at him.* ELMER *quietly infolds her with his left arm, and seizes the right wrist of* BOSWORTH.)

*Elmer* (*fiercely*). Dare to profane her with thy dastard hand, and I'll tear — (*starting, and glancing at hand*). Ah! what is this? (*Steps in front of* RUTH,

5

*still grasping* BOSWORTH'S *wrist*.)    A blood-red scar across the hand (*looks inquiringly at* BOSWORTH'S *face*). Yes, yes, despite the shaven face, the Quaker garb, I know thee now, Richard Cross, my mother's murderer. (*Flings* BOSWORTH *back to* R.)

*Bosworth.*    'Tis false ; we never met until this day.

*Elmer.*    But once : the day you outraged mankind by a deed so coldly cruel that fiends would blush to own it.    For a year I have sought you, Richard Cross, in town and country, midst my country's foes ; ay, turned the dead upon the field of battle that I might find that bloody mark upon a lifeless hand and know my mother's murder was avenged.    At last we meet. Heaven has reserved thee for a son's avenging hand. Richard Cross, but one of us must quit this place alive. (*Approaches him.*)

*Bosworth* (*aloud*).    Stand back ! my friends are at my call.    Hallo, Burke !

*Elmer* (*seizing him by the throat*).    Too late ! too late !    Dog, you must die.

*Bosworth.*    Take off your hand !    (*Struggle.*)

*Ruth* (L.).    Elmer, forbear.    (ELMER *and* BOSWORTH, *who have been struggling, pause with their hands on each other.*)    Respect my father's roof.    This is a home of peace, let no unhallowed deed pollute its fair fame. Thy mother is an angel now ; and vengeance, by the will of heaven, wields its own power in the guilty breast, to punish and destroy.

*Elmer.*    You are right, Ruth.    This house shall be respected.    (*Flings* BOSWORTH *back* R.)    Richard Cross, the girl you have insulted saves you now ; but beware ! your fate is sealed whene'er we meet again.

*Bosworth.* And yours is already sealed. (*Takes a knife from his bosom, and rushes at* ELMER, C. ELMER *steps* R., *puts up his left arm, and receives the blow.*)

*Elmer* (*seizing his own left arm with his right*). Ah! (*Staggers to* R.)

*Bosworth* (*running up to door* L.) Curse the luck! Yet, though my hand has failed, you are doomed. Fool, you know me not; I *did* strike down your mother, and I glory in the deed. You have stepped between me and the woman there; but she is mine, and you this night shall keep your mother company. (*Exit door in flat.*)

*Ruth* (*running to* ELMER). Thee is sorely hurt, dear Elmer.

*Elmer.* Nay, 'tis but a scratch. (*Report of two guns in quick succession outside.*) Ah, what's that?

*Bosworth* (*outside*). Oh! Fools, you have slain your leader.

*Elmer.* Even so, the wretch has fallen into his own trap. You were right, Ruth: vengeance alone belongeth to Him. (*Enter door in flat,* EPHRAIM *with gun. He stands it beside window.*)

*Ephraim.* Yea, verily, Friend Bosworth lieth in the road, with two bullets in his body; and, in the language of the world's people, he is as dead as a door-nail. (*Enter* R., PRUDENCE. *She crosses to* L.)

*Prudence.* What on earth is all this racket about? (*Enter* OBED, L., *followed by* MRS. S.; *he in his shirt-sleeves; she with a short nightdress over dark petticoat, nightcap on her head.*)

*Obed.* Verily, the foe is upon us.

*Mrs. S.* Children, what does this mean?

*Elmer.* Simply, Friend Obed, that the wolf in sheep's clothing, known to you as Uriel Bosworth, has invaded your home with the design of carrying off your daughter.

*Ruth.* Yea, and the brave Friend Elmer hath defended thy daughter with an arm of power and a heart of steel.

*Obed.* Verily, we owe thanks to our brave defender, and our daughter will prize him as a dear friend.

*Elmer.* May I not hope to find a warmer place in your affections, Ruth?

*Ruth.* Yea, thee is so brave and powerful that no place thou wishest can be too strong for thee.

*Obed.* Yea, verily, this sounds very much like love (*groans*). What will the Friends say?

*Mrs. S.* Never thee trouble thyself about the Friends, Obed. The young people will settle their affairs without their aid.

*Ephraim* (L.). Yea, it is not good for man to be alone, and my heart warmeth to one of the fair sex among the world's people.

*Obed* (c.). Thou, Ephraim? Profanation upon profanation. (*Groans.*)

*Ephraim.* Yea, I have been taught the rules of war by her, and with her I would walk the flowery paths of peace. Her name is Prudence, and her features are comely.

*Prudence.* Well, I never! And you sacked me an hour ago.

*Ephraim.* Yea, and in sackcloth and ashes have I repented.

*Obed.* Verily, this is too much. We shall all be disowned. (*Groans.*) We would give our lamb to the sacrifice, and now —

*Mrs. S.* Verily, Obed, we might as well be hung for a sheep as a lamb.

*Obed.* Yea, verily. (*Groans.*)

(*Distant fife and drum heard; distant report of musketry, with cheers and ringing of bells.*)

*Ginger* (*outside*). Hooray! hooray! (*runs in door in flat*). D'ye hear dat? Dey's gone and done it. Yas indeed. Down dar to Filledel. Dey's 'dopted de declamation of jurisprudence; an' —' an — de country am free. Yas it am. By golly, I's gwine to make one explosion. (*Runs to window, throws it up, takes gun, points it out, and fires; gun kicks him over on to floor.*) We'se free! we'se free!

*Pretzel* (*outside*). Oh, mine gracious, mine het pes plown into der mittle of der week pefore next. (*Enters door in flat holding on to his head.*)

*Ginger.* Golly, dat ar Tuchman's for ebber and ebber layin' round loose.

*Pretzel* (*comes down*). Mine het is full of pullets, unt mine prains is full of mine poots.

*Ginger.* Yah, yah! dat ain't nuffin, Massa Pretzel; dat's only a salute (*goes down extreme* L.).

*Pretzel* (*goes down* R.). Salute? Dot's vat you call him. He purn my eyeprows off mit his nonsense. Dot is no goot.

*Ginger.* Burn your eyebrows off; yah, yah! Yas, so you can see de glorious orb of liberty breaking —

*Pretzel.* Yaw, let him preak; he don't owe me sometings pretty much.     **5\***

*Elmer* (*takes Ruth to* c.). Yes, the day of liberty is breaking. The title-deed to a land of freedom has this day been taken by patriots whose dauntless valor shall rouse a people to battle against the invaders of our soil, until pæans of victory shall ring from shore to shore, and peace, with all its joys, nestle contented in the protecting arms of a free and powerful nation.

C.

ELMER.   RUTH.

R.        OBED.                    EPHRAIM.            L.

MRS. S.                          PRUDENCE.

PRETZEL.                                GINGER.

(*Red fire behind flat for bonfire; bells ringing, guns firing, people shouting. Curtain.*)

www.ingramcontent.com/pod-product-compliance
Lightning Source LLC
Chambersburg PA
CBHW022039080426
42733CB00007B/898